EFFECTIVE MEETINGS

20 Sure-Fire Tools

Volume 2 of The Parker Team Series

"A successful meeting is not measured by starting on time, having a great agenda, getting everyone involved, or even serving healthy muffins. While all these factors are important..."

...a great meeting is quite simply one that *achieves its objectives*— in other words, where a problem is solved, a decision is made, a plan is developed, a question is answered, or some other specific outcome is accomplished."

– Glenn Parker

GLENN PARKER

HRD Press, Inc. • Amherst • Massachusetts

This publication draws heavily on materials in *Meeting Excellence: 33 Tools to Lead Meetings that Get Results* by Glenn Parker & Robert Hoffman (Wiley, 2006).

Published by: HRD Press, Inc.
                 22 Amherst Road
                 Amherst, MA 01002
                 1-800-822-2801
                 413-253-3488
                 413-253-3490 (fax)
                 www.hrdpress.com

ISBN 978-1-59996-176-7

Editorial Services:
Production Services: Jean S. Miller
Cover Design: Eileen Klockars

TO MEET OR NOT TO MEET

That is the question. Whether 'tis nobler to suffer the slings and arrows of a useless meeting than to take action and simply call it off. Sometimes the best meeting is the meeting that didn't happen. Sometimes the best decision you can make is to cancel or postpone your meeting.

Just because your development team is scheduled to meet every Thursday morning doesn't mean that it has to take place. There is no rule that says just because your customer service department gets together every Monday morning that you can't skip it this week.

If you think of a meeting as an investment—an investment of the time and energy of the members of your team, you may decide that a meeting will not produce a worthwhile return on that investment. Think about it—you are investing the talents of 10 people for a period of two hours. Is the expected outcome produced by those people during that time sufficiently valuable for the organization? Perhaps their time might be better spent elsewhere.

The rule of thumb is:

No Purpose = No Meeting

> "Oh, how precious is time, and how it pains me to see it slide away, while I do so little to any good purpose."
>
> *– David Brainard*

To meet or not to meet...
...*these* are the questions

1. *Is there a real reason to meet?* Developing a set of responses to questions raised by the legal department is a specific purpose for a meeting. Deciding on a new vendor for the project is a useful purpose. However, simply reviewing reports from field staff may not be a legitimate reason for a meeting.

2. *Is now the best time to meet?* Next Monday may not be the best time to meet if a key player is out of town, the survey data will not be available for another week or a reorganization affecting all of the team members will be announced this week.

3. *Would something else work better than a full team meeting?* If the purpose of the meeting is simply to get an update on the project, it might be better to just send everyone an electronic copy of the report. If a problem requires the input of only a few members of the team, an informal get-together in an office may be the best choice. If the leader needs information from some members, walking around to their office or a telephone conversation may be a better alternative than a team meeting.

4. *What if the meeting was canceled?* What would be lost? Would team members or management be unhappy? If the answer is that "nothing would be lost" or "everyone would be very happy," then you have your answer.

PREPARE, PREPARE, PREPARE

You are ready for this meeting. You have done all the right things.

- You prepared the agenda and you sent it out a few days before the meeting.

- All the necessary documents were sent to the members or posted on the team space.

- The meeting room has been reserved or the teleconference number is set.

- Even the refreshments have been ordered.

All the necessary preparation is complete—or is it?

Even though the pre-meeting mechanics are in place, getting ready for the meeting should involve some additional work.

One critical way to prepare for success is to check with the key players on the agenda. For example, if one person is responsible for a presentation that will serve as the basis for an important decision, ensure that she is ready and even offer to help, if necessary. Similarly, if a member is tasked with an action item that supports an important agenda item, check to see if he will be ready to report.

> "The best preparation for tomorrow is to do today's work superbly well."
>
> — *William Osler*

3

Prepare, Prepare, and Prepare Some More

A few minutes thinking about the meeting in advance may eliminate problems during the meeting, and result in a successful meeting. Here are some tips:

- **How will you make decisions?** If the agenda includes a decision on a key aspect of the project, how will you make the decision—consensus, majority vote, or another way?

- **Review Your Ground Rules.** If you have ground rules, will it help to review the ones that pertain to an issue that may come up at the meeting? For example, if you expect some contention over a particular issue on the agenda, it might help to review the ground rules on resolving conflicts.

- **Check Attendance.** A few days before the meeting, check the responses to see who is attending. If a key meeting outcome depends upon the participation and support of certain members, are those people planning to attend? For example, if a critical agenda item focuses on the launch of a new sales training program, will both the sales and training people be there? It is obviously better to know this information in advance, when you can make adjustments, then to learn it at the start of the meeting when your options are limited.

- *Play "What if?"* Play a little mental game with yourself that visualizes possible problem situations and how you will handle them. For example:

  ✓ What if a senior manager shows up unexpectedly?

  ✓ What if the meeting starts 20 minutes late?

  ✓ What if a key player gets sick at the last minute?

  ✓ What if the equipment does not work?

  ✓ What if only a small percentage of the expected people show up?

  ✓ What if two key members get into an argument over a key outcome?

"Plans are nothing. Planning is everything."

– *Dwight D. Eisenhower*

CREATE AN ACTION AGENDA

Many people believe that what you do prior to the meeting determines the potential for a successful meeting. It's all in the planning.

And the key planning tool is the agenda—what I call the *Action Agenda.* One of the biggest complaints that people have about their meetings is that they "get off track." Well, in order to get back on track, you need to have a track and the meeting track is the agenda. What people are really saying is "let's get back on the agenda."

Keys to an effective action agenda include:

- *Key Meeting Outcome.* This is the main purpose of the meeting. If you only accomplish this one thing during your meeting, you can probably call it a successful meeting. It could be a decision that needs to be made, a problem that requires a solution, a plan that must be developed and other similar important outcomes.

- *Pre-Meeting Preparation.* This is the "homework" that is required for the meeting, such as reading a key document, collecting some data, thinking about an issue or discussing a topic with your manager.

- *Specific Topics.* Agenda items should be as specific as possible, e.g., rather than "project update" say "develop a plan for feasibility testing of the ABXY project."

- *Time Estimates.* Effective meeting planning includes an estimate of how long it will take to complete each agenda item.

- *Action Required.* It is useful to tell team members what action is necessary for each agenda item. In other words, will they need to make a decision or review a report?

- *Who is Responsible.* Someone should "own" each agenda item, i.e., facilitate the discussion, answer questions, present findings, etc.

Finally, our rule of thumb is that *agenda items are listed in order of importance.* In most cases, this means that the key meeting outcome is the first item on the agenda.

Meeting Notice and Agenda

Meeting Title: ABXY Project Meeting

Meeting Date: April 30

Starting Time: 2:00 p.m.   **Ending Time:** 3:15 p.m.

Location: Conference Room A

Pre-Work: Read first quarter budget report; read customer survey executive summary; review March meeting minutes; think about value-added of a new district

Key Meeting Outcome: Develop a revised budget for the project.

Agenda

Topic	Action	Responsibility	Time
Status of Budget: Plan vs. Actual	Create a revised project budget	J. Kaplan	30 min.
Creation of new work district	Decision	V. Ku	20 min.
Feedback from customers	F.Y.I.	S. Edwards	15 min.
Presentation at ACM conference	Who will prepare?	A. Carlin	10 min.

"In the real world, agendas are as rare as the white rhino and, if they do exist, they're about as useful."

– *Michael Schrage*

AGREE ON GROUND RULES

Norms, or ground rules as they are often known, are the "rules of engagement" for team members. Norms tell you how you are supposed to conduct yourself as a team member. Teams establish ground rules because if they don't, norms will develop anyway, and some may be counterproductive.

For example, people often tell me, "Our meetings always start late." What they have just told me is that an informal ground rule about showing up on time has developed and people are living by it. So, the preferred course of action is to establish a set of positive rules that you want to live by.

Norms tell each member of the team that you are expected to act in a certain way. And if we all live by these rules, there is a good chance we will have an effective team.

More specifically, our meetings will go better if we agree on norms about meeting behavior. Meeting norms serve two purposes:

1. They tell you what is expected of you as a meeting participant ("inform the team leader if I am unable to attend the meeting").

2. They provide a basis for members to give each other feedback when live by or violate a norm ("Jonathan, do you remember that we said there would be no multitasking during the meeting, including checking e-mail?")

While we provide you here with a list of sample meeting norms, it works best if your team decides on their specific norms. It's important that team members "own" the norms, because they are more likely to live by rules that they have had a hand in developing.

Once you have established your meeting norms, post them in a prominent place such as all your conference rooms and include the list in every meeting notice and in the set of materials provided to all new team members, until they become ingrained.

"The rules which experience suggest are better than those which the theorists elaborate."

– R. S. Storrs

Sample Meeting Norms

As a member of this team, I will...

- Show up on time for all meetings.

- Read the agenda and come prepared to discuss the issues and, where appropriate, make a decision on the issues.

- Inform the team leader if I am unable to attend the meeting.

- Provide the team leader with any outstanding action items or requested input on agenda items if I am unable to attend the meeting.

- Ask questions for clarification when I do not understand an issue.

- Actively listen to all sides of an issue in an effort to reach a consensus.

- Be brief and get to the point.

- Provide realistic due dates for my action items and deliverables.

- Focus only on the agenda items and not multi-task, such as reading and responding to emails.

> "In football, as in life, you must learn to play within the rules of the game."
>
> – *Hayden Fry*

THE KICK-OFF MEETING

GETTING OFF ON THE RIGHT FOOT

For some teams, the first meeting of a new team *is* the kick-off meeting. However, I believe that a kick-off meeting is a specific event or activity that has some really specific components.

The purpose of an effective team kick-off meeting is to:

- Clarify management's expectations of the team, including any limitations or items that are not negotiable.

- Present the overarching goal or purpose of the team, including any due dates or deliverables that are not subject to change.

- Identify the roles played by the members of the team in a general way.

- Respond to the concerns and questions members have about the team and their role such as:

  - I am already on three other teams. How important is this team in relation to the other three?

  - This project's deadline looks challenging. Will we be able to get additional resources to help us?

  - Why don't we have someone from the _____ department on the team?

- Start the process of members getting to know each other. At a minimum, ask everyone to introduce themselves, telling the group about their background, experience, skills, past projects, and how they expect to be able to help this team, as well as about their hobbies, interests and other ways they spend their time outside of work.

- Create a draft of the team's charter or project plan.

"The way you start is an excellent predictor of how you will end."

— Glenn Parker

Sample Kick-off Meeting Agenda

Name of Team: ABXY Project Meeting

Meeting Date: April 30

Starting Time: 9:30 a.m.   **Ending Time:**   11:30 a.m.

Location: Conference Room A

Pre-Work: Meet with your manager to discuss the project, your role in relation to other current assignments; prepare a list of questions and concerns you have about the team and the project.

Key Meeting Outcome: Understand management's expectations for the project; identify the goal of the project; meet your teammates; clarification of members' concerns and questions.

Agenda

Topic	Action	Responsibility	Time
Introduction of team members	Meet teammates	Hans	15 min.
Overview of new project	Agreement on initial plan	Hans	20 min.
Management's expectations of the team and project	Clarification and questions	Erika	15 min.
Your concerns and questions	Responses by leader and manager	Hans and Erika	30 min.
Draft of team charter	Preliminary agreement	All	30 min.
Presentation at ACM conference	Who will prepare?	A. Carlin	10 min.

Part 1: Before the Meeting

When we typically think of time management for meetings, we usually think of what happens during the meeting. In other words, the focus is "keeping on track" during the meeting. However, it is equally important to consider the time management issues that you can control during the planning stage prior to the meeting. Such time management issues include:

- What is the best day of the week for a meeting?
- What is the best time of day for a meeting?
- How long should a meeting run?
- Should you take breaks during a meeting?
- Is a working lunch meeting effective?

Let's tackle these issues.

When to Meet
Monday afternoon - Friday morning
9:30 a.m. - 12:00 noon
2:30 p.m. - 5:00 p.m.

When Not to Meet
Avoid Monday morning
Avoid Friday afternoon
Avoid right after lunch

How Long to Meet
Ideal = 1 hour
Acceptable = 1.5 hours
Unacceptable = Over 2 hours

Breaks
One per hour
Length = 10 minutes
Use "stretch" breaks
Allow members to call breaks

"I am definitely going to take a course in time management just as soon as I can work it into my schedule."

– *Louis E. Boone*

The Great Working Lunch Meeting Debate

Meet Positive Petra:

"While I would not want to meet every day for a working lunch, I do like it occasionally as a nice break from the usual routine. Last year, for example, the Oncor Project Team began with a kick-off meeting during the noon hour which included a nice buffet lunch.

In this case, the working lunch was very effective because it gave us some time to talk informally about the project and get to know our teammates in a social atmosphere. When the meeting officially started, the "ice had been broken" and everyone was in a good mood.

At other times, we needed to pull together a meeting on short notice to give members a quick update on an important and urgent development. In a number of these cases, we found that having a lunch meeting was the best, most efficient thing to do. As long as the food was good and the meeting was over in about an hour, it was just fine."

The Great Working Lunch Meeting Debate

Meet Negative Nellie:

"I resent lunch meetings. The lunch break is my time. I use the time to renew and refresh myself for the rest of the day. I also use the time to take care of some personal business that I cannot get done at the end of the business day. Here are some of the ways I have used my lunch break:

- Socialize with a colleague over lunch in the cafeteria
- Take an exercise walk around the campus
- Run some local errands
- Catch up on some of my reading
- Do some online banking and other related chores
- Call my babysitter to see about my daughter's cold"

Part 2: During the Meeting

In my research on corporate meetings, I found that during data collection interviews with team members that "getting off track," "wasting time," and "not accomplishing anything useful" were the biggest complaints.

The biggest problems are:

1. **Topic Migration.** Migration involves bringing up either an irrelevant topic or an intellectually challenging idea that is not on the agenda.

   Solution: One good way to address this problem is simply to intervene with a clear comment such as "It looks like we have drifted from the agenda topic. Let's get back to the agenda now and put this current discussion in the 'parking lot' for future consideration."

2. **Topic Magnification.** In this case, the topic is on the agenda but it is of great interest to only a few members who can go on discussing it at length while the remaining members have little or no interest. The net result is that the most of the members disengage and become observers or, worse, engage in various dysfunctional behaviors such as side conversations or checking their e-mail.

Solution: It is best to address this type of problem before the meeting by setting up a sub-group of interested members to discuss it. However, if it occurs during the meeting, stop and ask the sub-group to have an outside meeting and report back at the next full team meeting.

"There is never enough time to do it right, but there is always enough time to do it over."

— Jack Bergman

It's All About
Asking the Right Questions

As a meeting facilitator, you must master the art of asking a good question. In addition, it is important to develop a wide repertoire of questions. For example, we often see team leaders using that tired old question—"does anyone have any questions?"—again and again. In addition to being a simple "yes or no" question, it also sounds perfunctory when it used repeatedly, as if you really don't expect any questions and are just "going through the motions."

In the end, your goal in any team discussion is to utilize all the expertise in the room (or on the line) to accomplish the meeting's objectives. Here are the types of questions most often used by facilitators:

1. **Open-ended.** Most often starting with What, How or Why, this type of question cannot be answered with a yes or no. For example, "How will this problem impact our timeline?"

2. **Closed-end.** When you are looking for a direct and specific response, you ask a question that can only be answered with a yes or no, as in "Are we going to enter this market?"

3. **Overhead.** This is a question that is asked of the entire group so that anyone on the team can provide a response such as "What are some of the ways we can deal with this problem?"

4. **Direct.** Although used sparingly, there are some times when you can ask a team member a direct question; for example, "Judy, from a marketing perspective, what do you think we should do?'

5. **Re-direct.** Since you are trying to get people involved rather than dominate the discussion, when someone asks you a direct question, you can re-direct to a member of the team. Here's how it works: "That's an interesting question, Mario. What do you think about it?"

6. **Relay**. Alternatively, you can take a question directed to you and relay it to the whole team as an overhead question, as in "Jacques asks a good question, how do the rest of you feel about it?"

7. **Consensus.** You can use a question to test to see if the team has reached a consensus, as in the following example: "Am I correct saying that we have reached consensus on going with this new vendor for this project?"

> "The greatest gift is not being afraid to ask a question…."
>
> *— Ruby Dee*

Tips for a Terrific Teleconference

As companies go global and teams go global, face-to-face meetings become too costly because of travel expenses. As a result, more and more meetings are held via teleconference. A teleconference is attractive because it is easy to set up, the technology rarely breaks down and it is inexpensive. The audio-only limitation of the teleconference can be augmented by various web-based tools, such as WebEx from Cisco, that allows you to view a slide, brainstorm or comment using a whiteboard, see a list of meeting participants and send instant messages to each other.

Teleconferences vary according to where the participants are located. In some cases, a group in one location is seated around a conference table with a large speakerphone, while a similar group is at another location, while some other individual team members are calling in from their office or hotel on a handset or cell phone.

As a facilitator, you can ensure your teleconference meeting is a success by:

- Sending out the agenda and related materials prior to the meeting.

- Arriving early to ensure the teleconference support is operating and to greet people as they come on the line.

- Starting on time or no later than five minutes after the designated start time.

- Asking each person to identify themselves and their location.

- Reviewing the agenda, key meeting outcome and, as appropriate, the meeting norms.

- Ask people to identify themselves before they speak.

- If some people have not spoken, try bringing them into the discussion with something like, "Judy, from a regulatory perspective, what are the questions we need to be prepared for?"

- On important decisions, call on each person to ensure they agree with the decision.

> "If we discovered we only had five minutes left to say all we wanted to say, every telephone would be in use by people telling other people how much they loved them."
>
> — *Author Unknown*

What to Do About Silent Sam

He just doesn't want to be there. He is quiet, reserved, maybe just an introvert. He likes working with things and ideas. He is not a people person and hates meetings. He sits in these teleconference meetings and thinks about how much work he has to do and how much time he is wasting sitting here.

And yet, the team needs his expertise as they tackle this new product opportunity.

As the team leader, what can you do about Sam? Here are some options:

- **Make Him an Adjunct Member.** Why make him sit through all these meetings when you only need his expertise at specific times? As an adjunct member, he needs only to attend certain meetings.

- **Be Supportive**. When Sam does say something, offer a supportive comment such as "Thanks Sam, that's a good thought. How do the rest of you feel about Sam's suggestion that we move in a different direction?"

- **Call on Him**. This can be tricky but it works if handled carefully. Pick a topic that allows Sam to share his expertise with something like, "Sam, I know you have had experience in evaluating IT systems. What are some of the ways we can make our systems more user friendly?"

- **Tell Him in Advance You Will Call on Him.** Speak with Sam outside of the meeting and let him know that you expect to call on him to share his expertise during the meeting. This will give him an opportunity to prepare his remarks.

- **Ask Him to Take on an Action Item.** And after the meeting, ask if you can help with either the research on the action item or the presentation at the meeting.

"I assume that silence gives consent."

– Plato

FACILITATING A CROSS-CULTURAL MEETING

There are many things that can go wrong in a meeting. This booklet is intended to deal with many of these things. However, one area that is often overlooked—maybe because it is considered too sensitive—is communicating across language differences in a meeting. Since most business meetings are conducted in English, the issue becomes how to use the language in a way that facilitates clear communication rather than serve as a barrier. While we understand that cultural communication involves other things such as nonverbal cues (e.g., eye contact, space) and protocol (speaking directly to a superior), the focus of this tool is solely on language in the context of a meeting.

Tips for Meeting Facilitators:

- *Stop team members when they use sports analogies, colloquial expressions and unfamiliar jargon.* When you hear someone refer to a new procedure as a "slam dunk," stop and ask for an explanation of the phrase in the context of the issue under consideration.

- *Be diligent about periodically summarizing decisions and action items.* Use your active listening skills to capture agreements with something like, "It looks like we have consensus on the wording of our response to management's query."

- *Tactfully interrupt members during a long statement with a paraphrase of each key point.* You can make it easier for everyone to understand what is being said if it is presented in small segments. A good facilitator intervention is "Hans, you make a good point, so let me stop and make sure everyone understands that you believe we should get trained in the new system as soon as possible."

- *Don't simply ask, "Do you all understand?"* People will rarely admit they do not understand since it implies that they incompetent. Instead, use your active listening skills as suggested above.

- In a face-to-face meeting, look for nonverbal signs such as frowns, eye rolling or head shaking that indicate the person does not understand.

> "If the English language made any sense, lackadaisical would have something to do with a shortage of flowers."
>
> *— Doug Larsen*

BEWARE! Hazardous to Cross-Cultural Communication

Colloquial Expressions:

- This opportunity is going to vanish *into thin air*
- He is *full of hot air.*
- After the announcement, *all hell broke loose.*
- This whole marketing team was *up in arms.*
- I could feel my *ears burning.*
- I am *all ears.*
- Her presentation really *laid an egg.*
- They are *in cahoots* with the vendor.
- It's a *piece of cake.*
- Let's *call a spade a spade.*
- If we *play our cards right*, we can get this contract.

Sports Analogies:

- Let's *beat them to the punch.*
- He was *way off base.*
- Don't *make waves.*
- You need to *fish or cut bait.*
- This is going to be *a long shot.*
- We are *skating on thin ice.*
- I think we need to *call an audible.*
- This is a real *wild card.*
- Don't look a *gift horse in the mouth.*
- We should *call their bluff.*

HANDLING CONFLICTS IN A TEAM MEETING

Conflicts, or more precisely, differences of opinion, are a natural part of a team meeting, especially of a cross-functional team meeting. When you bring people together who have different backgrounds, experiences, styles, training and goals, you expect and want differences because you believe that the best decisions emerge when all points of view are considered. While conflicts are desirable, more important for an effective meeting is the ability to resolve those differences in a professional manner.

Types of Conflicts in Meetings:

1. **Decisions:** What are we going to do?
2. **Direction:** Where are we going?
3. **Priorities:** What is most important?
4. **Process:** How are we going get it done?

Tools for Resolving Conflicts in Meetings:

- *Manage the Discussion.* Facilitate the interaction toward a reasoned solution.

- *Don't Deny or Smooth Over.* Don't allow people to minimize the issue.

- *Ensure Understanding.* Help people grasp all sides of the issue.

- *Clarify Alternatives.* Explain different suggestions and recommendations.

- *Avoid Jumping to a Quick Solution.* Control the urge for a fast fix.

- *Break into Parts.* Consider dividing the problem into manageable elements.

- *Defuse Anger.* Do not allow people to get angry at each other.

> "A positive attitude may not solve all of your problems but it will annoy enough people to make it worth the effort."
>
> *– Herm Albright*

Learning How to Resolve Conflicts in a Meeting

A Training Exercise

Resources Needed

- *Dealing with Conflict Instrument (DCI)* booklet for each person. Order from www.hrdpress.com

- *Dealing with Conflict* video. Order from www.hrdpress.com

Design

1. Facilitate a brainstorming session of "typical conflicts in your team meetings."

2. Eliminate duplicates and overlaps. Prioritize the list in order of frequency.

3. Ask each person to complete the *DCI* survey and score the results.

4. Show the video.

5. Present a description of the various conflict modes. Facilitate a discussion with the goal of clarifying and understanding each style. The instrument contains a description of each of the styles.

6. Return to the "typical conflicts" and the top three types of conflicts on the prioritized list.

7. Divide into subgroups to discuss (a) what mode was used in each situation, and (b) what would you do differently now as a result of learning about various conflict resolution styles.

8. Conclude the session by developing a list of team ground rules for resolving conflicts in the future.

We have all experienced people on our teams or in meetings who, at various times, engage in dysfunctional behavior. They disrupt your meetings in a variety of ways, including monopolizing the discussion, being rude to their colleagues and pushing their personal agenda.

Who are these people? Here is our gallery of meeting monsters. Have you ever seen these characters in your meetings?

- **Silent Sam.** This person sits through your meeting without uttering a word or in any other way contributing to the goals of the meeting. In a face-to-face meeting, you often see facial expressions that indicate that he would just rather not be there.

- **Morris the Monopolizer.** Just the opposite of Silent Sam, this person talks too much. He likes to hear the sound of his voice and has no interest in hearing anything from anyone else in the meeting. He usually thinks that he knows more than anyone else or is the only one with something to say on the topic.

- **Contessa the Contrarian.** She is against everything and everybody and never contributes a positive thought to the meeting. She seems to enjoy being against whatever is presented or proposed. The Contrarian is not to be confused with the Challenger, who raises important questions for the team to consider in an effort to achieve their objectives.

- **Tangent Tom**. He is the person who loves to discuss anything except the items on the agenda. So, he will try to take the discussion to some topic that is of great interest to him but is not relevant to the goals of the meeting, and often not relevant to the goals of the team.

- **Nasty Nellie**. She is rude and disrespectful to colleagues, often engaging in condescending remarks and exhibiting negative nonverbal facial expressions. She has the capacity to make others feel that their contributions are either stupid, unwelcome, or both.

"People achieve more working with others than against them."

– Allan Fromme

Managing Your Monsters

So, you have a monster in your meeting. And you're ready to do something about it. Here are some tips:

1. **Address Their Actions, not Their Personality.** Discuss what they did, not who they are. "When you consistently come late to our meetings and sit silently with your arms folded . . .:" It's a lot easier to change behavior than personality.

2. **Don't Jump to Conclusions.** If Jonas comes late to a meeting and sits silently throughout the meeting, there is no reason to address his behavior at this point. He may have just come from another meeting where there were problems, or just found out he has to be out of town and will miss his son's birthday, or maybe he's just having a bad day. You only want to take action when the behavior occurs multiple times over the course of several meetings.

3. **Be Open to Alternatives.** It is just possible that what you see as dysfunctional behavior is really an expression of an alternative style that you may not appreciate. For example, what you see as persistent negative behavior is really Contessa simply being an effective Challenger who is raising important questions that the team needs to consider. If you are unsure, check with some of your teammates before you act.

4. **Refer to Your Norms.** The best (and safest) way to manage your monster is to bring out your meeting norms. "Jonas, as you may remember, one of our most important norms is 'show up on time for all meetings.' You have been late for our last three

meetings. What is going on, and what can I do to help to ensure that you arrive on time for our next meeting?"

5. **Have a Private Conversation.** It is always best to have any discussion of dysfunctional behavior in private. The atmosphere is more likely to be calm and the person will be more willing to address the issue.

6. **Highlight Positive Actions.** When your monster does exhibit changed behavior, make sure to give her some positive reinforcement: "Contessa, thanks for your helpful additions to Jonas' report."

"Success or failure in business is caused by mental attitude even more than by mental capacities."

— Walter Scott

DECISIONS, DECISIONS...

In many ways, teams, or at least effective teams, come together to make decisions. Meetings are primarily a forum to make decisions. We may cloak it in different terms such as solving a problem, developing a plan or choosing a vendor but, in the end, these actions are all decisions that need to be made and most of them are made in a meeting. In fact, we say that unless you have to make a decision, there is really no reason to meet. A meeting gives team members an opportunity to ensure that:

- All members have a chance to participate in the process.

- Everyone understands all sides of the issue.

- The decision is consistent with the team's purpose and with the overarching goals of the organization.

- All members support the decision and are willing to help implement it.

Decision-Making Methods

1. **Autocratic.** "We are going to open three new sites in the Asia/Pacific region."

2. **Participative.** "Although I am ultimately responsible for this one, I need your input on where we should locate these sites."

3. **Expert.** "This is a decision that we are going to leave to Jeff, since the rest of us know very little about the demographics of the area."

4. **Democratic.** "Since we have been asked to decide on the location of the sites, how many of you think one of the sites should be set up in a rural village? How many agree with Jeff that all three sites should be located in the largest urban areas?"

5. **Consensus.** "While it sounds like some of you still have reservations, everyone is agreed that all three sites should be located in the largest urban areas in order to reach the largest number of people."

"A great leader is not a searcher for consensus but a molder of consensus."

— *Martin Luther King, Jr.*

Tips for Reaching a Consensus

1. *Clarify the Decision That Has to be Made.* "By the end of this meeting, we must decide on a vendor to implement these three new sites in the Asia/Pacific region."

2. *Clarify the Decision-Making Method.* "Because this decision requires the full commitment of all team members, I recommend that we strive for a consensus."

3. *Remind the Team About the Norms Concerning Consensus.* "Let me begin by reminding you that our norms for a consensus included allowing everyone an opportunity to participate in the discussion, to consider all points of view, agreeing on a decision you can live with (even if you have some concerns about it) and finally, a willingness to work hard to implement the decision."

4. *Take a Look at the Advantages and Disadvantages of the Various Options.* "Before we try to reach a consensus, let's hear about the pros and cons of each of the alternatives, so we can make an informed choice."

5. *When it appears that there is some agreement among team members, throw out a possible consensus statement to see if the group really agrees and is ready to move on.* "All right, we have discussed these various possibilities and now it seems that we can all agree that we should locate these new sites in the three most-populated urban areas."

6. *If the decision is extremely important (or if this is a teleconference), you probably should poll the group to ensure everyone is really in agreement.* "Okay, I'd like to be sure that we have a true consensus by going around and asking each person if they agree. Suzanne, do you agree? Blair, can you live with it? . . ."

7. *End the process by developing a list of next steps for implementing the decision.* "Now that we have a consensus, let's come up with the action items necessary to implement it."

> "America is a place where we all come together. It is a place of consensus."
>
> — *Charles Schumer*

SPICE UP YOUR MEETINGS

Sometimes, despite your best efforts, meetings can become just plain dull. While most teams in business deal with serious issues such as sales, finance, marketing, products, services, and customers, adding a little fun can make it all go better.

In the end there is a serious purpose to fun. Since we know that people do their best work in an atmosphere that is informal and relaxed, it is important that we do what we can to facilitate the creation and maintenance of a positive climate. Studies show that when people are relaxed, the net result is more creative solutions, thoughtful decisions, and innovative ideas. The key is to make the activity short and easy-to-understand.

So, what can we do to spice up our meetings? Here are some possibilities:

1. *Fun Food.* Not all food is fun, but when you surprise people with snacks, for example, that are new or unexpected, it can encourage conversation. How about asking members of the team to bring in something that is representative of their culture, or simply their favorite recipe?

2. *Introductions.* Any simple activity that helps people get to know each other better helps establish a more positive climate. For example, ask team members to share their favorite vacation.

3. *Games.* A simple, but playful game can get people working together (not against each other) in a way that is fun for all. One easy activity that I have used involves giving the team a list of famous quotes (e.g.,

"Success is getting up one more time than you fall")
and asking the team to decide which quote best
represents our team (or our customers or industry).

4. **Toys.** Small items such as soft squeeze balls, Nerf
   balls or noise makers are great to give people to play
   with at the beginning of a meeting. You make it
   interactive by tossing a ball to the next person on the
   agenda, or to someone you want to get involved in the
   discussion.

> "For me, one of the most beautiful sounds
> in the world is a hearty laugh."
>
> — *Bennett Cerf*

Serious Fun at Team Meetings

- *Chocolate, Chocolate, Chocolate, and More Chocolate.*
  Provide the team with an all chocolate snack and drink
  table. Include chocolate cookies, chocolate brownies,
  chocolate cake, chocolate candy, chocolate pudding, and
  various chocolate drinks. It will create a lot of conversation and some happy team members.

- *Baby Face.* Before the meeting, ask everyone for one of
  their baby pictures. At the meeting, post the photos on
  the wall (or send them out attached to the meeting
  notice). Then ask people to try to match the photos with
  members of the team.

- *Brain Games.* Pick up a little book called *Brain Bafflers*
  by Robert Steinwachs for some short, fun games to liven
  up a meeting. For example:

  ➣ How do you take one from nineteen and still have
    twenty? (use Roman numerals: XIX and XX).

  ➣ Name ten cities (only one per country) starting with
    the letter "M" that have more than a million people
    living in them (Miami, Milan, Mexico City, Moscow,
    Manila, etc.)

  ➣ Unscramble these letters and make one word from
    them: OERWNDO (one word).

- *Sources for Meeting Toys:*

  ➣ www.trainerswarehouse.com

  ➣ www.creativelearningtools.com

CLOSING ON A POSITIVE NOTE

You opened the meeting by stating the key meeting outcome, reviewing the agenda and setting a positive tone. It was professional and positive and resulted in many useful accomplishments.

Now it's time to close out the meeting with same level of professionalism and in the same upbeat manner.

It should only take a few minutes, but an effective closing has many benefits for the team:

1. Members leave the meeting with a sense of accomplishment.

2. Members leave with a sense that their time has been well spent.

3. Members leave with clarity about key decisions and other agreements made during the meeting.

4. Members leave with a clear understanding of what they need to communicate to their managers and other stakeholders.

5. Members leave with a clear understanding of the action items for which they are responsible.

6. Members leave the meeting motivated to take action designed to accomplish the team's goals.

> "Why can't we get all the people together in the world that we really like and then just stay together? I guess that wouldn't work. Someone would leave. Someone always leaves. Then we would have to say goodbye. I hate goodbyes. I know what I need. I need more hellos."
>
> – Snoopy

51

Steps to an Effective Closing

1. Review the major decisions, agreements and other actions of the meeting.

2. Review the new action items.

3. Review the open action items.

4. Take note of the team's progress toward its objectives and how the outcomes of this meeting moved the team forward toward those objectives.

5. Set (or remind the team of) the date and time of the next meeting.

6. Evaluate the meeting.

7. Thank the members, especially the members who made special contributions to the success of the meeting.

"All's well that ends well."

– 15th Century English Proverb, Author Unknown

MEETING EVALUATION

HOW WAS IT FOR YOU?

Of all the things that we recommend for effective meeting management, the one area that is most often ignored, avoided or disliked is meeting evaluation. Most people will say that it is a good idea, that they should do it, then say they will do it, but then, somehow, it doesn't happen.

So, why don't people evaluate their meetings?

1. **It takes too much time.** It takes some time, but you can do it in just a few minutes by asking one or two simple questions, such as "What went well in today's meeting?" and "What can we do to improve our next meeting?" Alternatively, you can send out an e-mail survey after the meeting (improve your chances of getting people to respond by telling them at the end of the meeting to expect a brief survey in the next few days).

2. **We don't know what to ask.** All evaluation questions are variations on two themes: (a) what is going well in our meetings and should be continued, and (b) what should we do to improve our meetings in the future.

3. **We don't want to know what people think about the meetings (especially if people don't like the meetings).** Yes, you may get your feelings hurt if people do not like the meetings, but they may actually like the meetings and you need to know that so you can continue on the same path. However, if they don't like some things about your meetings, the only way to

change that is to find out what's wrong and then fix it. For the most part, members of your team will appreciate that you asked and will especially like it if you do something with their comments to improve future meetings.

4. **The members will dislike me for extending the time of the meeting.** It does take some courage to do the very first meeting evaluation and you might meet with some resistance. However, being a good leader means persevering against opposition when your goal is meaningful.

"To act coolly, intelligently, and prudently in perilous circumstances is the test of a man."

— Adlai Stevenson

Some Quick and Easy Evaluation Tools

Brainstorming

In a face-to-face meeting with access to a flip chart or in a teleconference with access to an online whiteboard, place a plus (+) sign at the top of the left column and a delta (^) at the top of the right column. Explain that under the plus column we will list positive aspects of the meeting, while under the delta column we will list aspects that should be changed. Then encourage meeting participants to simply throw out ideas for each list. If time permits, summarize the key conclusions.

Open Discussion

Present and/or post two questions: (1) How satisfied are you with the way this meeting was planned and carried out, and (2) How can our future meetings be improved? Facilitate the discussion for a few minutes and then summarize the key themes.

Survey Questionnaire

After the meeting, send an email to each person with a two-question survey about the effectiveness of the meeting. If you have access to a survey website such as www.zoomerang.com, use this service.

Here are two good questions:

1. How do you feel about what was accomplished at our previous meeting?

2. What suggestions do you have for our next meeting?

Here is another alternative:

1. How satisfied were you with yesterday's meeting? Please check one answer.

   ❏ Very satisfied
   ❏ Satisfied
   ❏ Dissatisfied
   ❏ Very dissatisfied

2. What can be done to improve our next meeting?

> "True genius resides in the capacity to evaluate uncertain, hazardous and conflicting information."
>
> — *Winston Churchill*

Notes, not minutes. Meeting minutes are a "written record" of everything that happened during the meeting, while notes are a summary of the key meeting outcomes. We recommend the use of notes with the more detailed documents attached to the notes or posted on the team's site.

In general, the purpose of meeting notes is to capture the highlights of the meeting, such as the major decisions and action items. Essentially, it is the highlights that the members and key stakeholders are most interested in seeing after the meeting.

The Essence

1. Date, time and location of the meeting

2. Names of members who attended (some teams also report the names of members who did not attend)

3. List of decisions and other key outcomes

4. List of action items: new, completed, and outstanding

5. Date, time, and location of the next meeting

6. List of attachments, including links to their location

Meeting Notes: A Sample

Date:

Members present:

Key Decisions and Outcomes:

1. The team agreed to present the new product plan at the next Executive Committee meeting.

2. The team decided to ask three vendors to present their approach to marketing *Concor* as part of an online strategy.

3. The team reached a consensus on a high level of dissatisfaction with the level of detail in the progress reports submitted by *IT Solutions.*

4. The team reviewed the deliverables due during the next quarter and agreed on the need to revise the plan given current market decisions.

Action	What	Who	When
Preparation of Product Plan Presentation	Prepare PPT Slides	Hans	October 1
Meet with Concor	Prepare	Robert, Alana, Jacques, Jim	Prior to 30 October
Revise Project Plan	Prepare	Melanie, Jonathan, Marla	October 16

Next meeting: October 30, 8:00 a.m. ET, teleconference (call-in number to be provided)

ACTION ITEM ACTION

We talked about what happens prior to the meeting as being an important predictor of the effectiveness of the meeting. Planning, we said, was critical to success. In much the same way, what happens after the meeting also determines the overall effectiveness of the meeting because it is at this time that meeting outcomes are implemented.

While so much of the focus of effective meetings emphasizes what takes place during the meeting, it is often the work done by members between meetings that is critical to successful meeting management and teamwork. And much of what happens between meetings involves work on action items generated during the meeting.

Surprisingly, action items have a way of building trust and general team morale. When members see their colleagues opting for follow-up tasks and committing to additional work in the form of action items, this reflects positively on team cohesion. And when members deliver on those action items, trust and team effectiveness increases even more.

High performing teams always do an excellent job of initiating, tracking and delivering on their action items. The effective use of action items means that teams use the precious time during meetings to set direction and make important decisions, and use the time outside of meetings to do the more time-consuming but necessary data collection and research required by the team.

> "Never confuse motion with action."
>
> *– Benjamin Franklin*

59

Ground Rules for Effective Action Items

1. Ensure all actions items include the work to be done, the date it is due and the person responsible for it.

2. When a new action item is identified during the meeting, clearly state the details.

3. If you have access to a flip chart or white board, write it out. If not, slowly and clearly state it ensuring that everyone, but especially the person responsible, understands it.

4. At the end of the meeting, review the list of action items.

5. As appropriate, indicate how the task supports the overall team goals.

6. Include the action items due in the meeting notice and agenda for the next meeting.

7. As appropriate, after the meeting, contact the person responsible to see if he or she needs help.

"Great managers have a bias for action."

– Tom Peters

IT AIN'T OVER EVEN AFTER IT'S OVER

You review the key decisions and action items. You even find time to conduct a brief evaluation of the meeting. You thank everyone for their contributions. It was a good meeting! You are finally done. Right? Wrong!

Hold on. Before you get ready for your next meeting, think about what you need to do to follow-up on this meeting. Follow-up is an important part of the total meeting process that began with all the planning and preparation that took place before the meeting and ends with a variety of post-meeting activities.

Here are a few after-meeting actions to consider:

- Review the notes and send them out to the team as soon as possible (some teams adopt a ground rule to cover this; for example, "notes will be distributed within 48 hours of the meeting").

- Communicate with your stakeholders about the key decisions and other relevant issues.

- Contact team members responsible for the important action items to ask if you can provide any assistance.

- Talk with any team members who appeared to have concerns or questions about decisions or anything else that took place during the meeting.

- Increase your credibility with the team by honoring any commitments you made during the meeting.

- Review the meeting evaluation to see if there are any changes you can implement at the next meeting.

- Spend a few minutes reflecting on your performance as the meeting facilitator.

Beware of the After Meeting "Meeting"

When the meeting ends, you stay around for a few minutes speaking to a few members, then gather up your belongings and head out the door of the conference room. As you leave the room, you notice a group of four people gathered together standing at the end of the corridor in what looks like an animated conversation. You have just come upon the "after meeting meeting."

When a meeting includes some contentious issues, when there are some strong feelings about a decision made at the meeting, or when there is lack of clarity about a topic that was discussed, the potential for this type of ad hoc meeting exists. These spontaneous meetings occur because:

- The climate in the meeting does not encourage or support free and open communication.

- One or two strong personalities dominate the discussion and intimidate other team members.

- The agenda does not include enough time to fully explore one or more agenda topics (sometimes you just cannot anticipate what issues will generate interest).

- Members are not happy with the way the meeting was planned and carried out.

- Members were not happy with a decision made at the meeting.

If you see such a meeting taking place or you hear that such a meeting took place, it is important to speak with the participants to identify the issues and determine how you can help. However, be prepared to accept some feedback and adjust your meeting facilitation style.

> "We bring together the best ideas—turning the meetings of our top managers into intellectual orgies."
>
> — *Jack Welch*

TRAINING FOR MEETING EFFECTIVENESS

Meeting effectiveness is a set of tools. We have covered most, if not all, of those tools in this publication. Meeting effectiveness is also a discipline. There are certain specific things you need to do every time in order to have a successful meeting. Meeting effectiveness is also a learned skill that is accompanied by knowledge of certain templates, protocols, and best practices.

Team leaders and managers can learn how to run better meetings, and team members can learn how to be more effective meeting participants. There are a number of ways of approaching learning in the area of meeting management, meeting facilitation, and meeting participation.

1. **Intact Team Building.** In this model, a functioning team, perhaps as part of an overall team-building intervention, analyzes the strengths and weaknesses of their meetings and then develops a plan for improvement. This approach is enhanced by the use of a survey instrument that provides data on the effectiveness of the team's meeting management. See the Resources on the next page for a reference to a meeting effectiveness survey. The value of this approach is that all members commit to supporting the implementation of the improvement plan.

2. **Meeting Facilitation Skills Training.** This is a classroom session designed for team and other meeting leaders. Depending upon the model, it almost always involves skill practice exercises where the participants facilitate a simulated meeting and then receive feedback from their peers and the instructor. If time permits, it may involve videotaping and feedback of the simulation.

3. **Meeting Management Class.** This approach is designed to reach a large population with the basic tools of effective meeting management. Therefore, it is usually an open enrollment class that may include both team leaders and team members (who may become leaders in the future). The curriculum includes a description and, as appropriate, examples and samples of best practices in successful meeting management. For example, it may provide a meeting agenda template and a set of sample meeting norms.

Resources for Meeting Effectiveness Training

Books

- G. Parker and R. Hoffman. *Meeting Excellence: 33 Tools to Lead Meetings That Get Results,* Wiley, 2006.

- R. Wright. *The Meeting Spectrum, 2ⁿᵈ Edition,* HRD Press, Inc., 2005.

- P. Savaghan, L. Goldstein, and C. Conway. *The Highly Effective Meeting Profile,* HRD Press, Inc., 2003.

- M. Silberman. *101 Ways to Make Meetings Active: Surefire Ideas to Engage Your Group,* Jossey-Bass/ Pfeiffer, 1999.

Articles

- E. Prewitt. "Pitfalls in Meetings and How to Avoid Them," *Harvard Management Update,* June 1998, pp. 3-5.

- E. Mason. "The Seven Sins of Deadly Meetings," *Fast Company,* April-May, 1996, p. 122.

Videos

- CRM Learning. *Meeting Robbers,* Revised Edition, undated.

- Kantola Productions. *Be Prepared for Meetings,* undated.

Web Sites

- www.effectivemeetings.com
- www.meetingwizard.org

Survey

- G. Parker. "Team Meeting Assessment," in G. Parker, *25 Instruments for Team Building*, HRD Press, Inc., 1998.

- P. Sanaghan, L. Goldstein and C. Conway. *The Highly Effective Meeting Profile*, HRD Press, Inc., 2003.

"I hated every minute of training, but I said 'Don't quit. Suffer now and live the rest of your life as a champion.'"

— Muhammad Ali

A Guide to Getting the Most from this Book

- **Read the Book.** Ask everyone to read the book and then ask, "If you could only select just one thing to do that would immediately improve our meetings, what would it be?" Facilitate a discussion of the answers.

- **Start with a Meeting Assessment.** Get the "Team Meeting Assessment" or some other meeting assessment instrument and ask everyone to complete it. Summarize the results and then facilitate a discussion focused on ways to improve your meetings in the future.

- **Facilitate an Informal Assessment.** At the end of a meeting, ask members to brainstorm things that are going well and should be continued and things that should be changed or added. When a few issues emerge, ask everyone to read those sections of this book. Then ask them to return to the next meeting with ideas for improving your meetings in the future.

- **Take One Step at a Time.** Devote 15-30 minutes of each meeting to a discussion of one of the tools in this book.

- **Let Members Take the Lead.** Ask each team member to take responsibility for leading a discussion on one of the 20 tools at a subsequent meeting.

- **Use the Book as a Pre-Program Assignment.** Get people thinking about meetings prior to attending a training session on the topic by reading this book and answering some questions.

- **Use the Book as a Follow-up Assignment.** Give this book out at the end of a program on meetings with an assignment to read the whole book or parts not covered during the training.

Glenn Parker

Author

As a consultant for more than 30 years, Glenn Parker has helped create high-performance teams at hundreds of organizations including Novartis Pharmaceuticals, Merck & Company, Philips-Van Heusen, Telcordia Technologies, BOC Gases, and the U.S. Coast Guard. He is an internationally-recognized workshop facilitator, organizational consultant, and conference speaker n the area of teamwork and team meetings.

Glenn is the author of some 16 books including several best-sellers such as *Team Players and Teamwork, Rewarding Teams: Lessons from the Trenches,* and *Cross Functional Teams: Working with Allies, Enemies and Other Strangers;* widely used instruments such as the *Parker Team Player Survey* and manuals for practitioners such as *50 Activities for Team Building, 25 Instruments for Team Building,* and *Team Workout: 50 Interactive Activities.*

His seminal work in team player styles was featured in the best-selling CRM video, *Team Building II: What Makes a Good Team Player?* Glenn is one of only 75 management thinkers recognize in the book, *The Guru Guide.* His latest book, *Meeting Excellence: 33 Tools to Lead Meetings that Get Results,* has been widely quoted and referenced in articles in the *New York Times, Forbes, CIO Magazine,* and others.

Glenn is the father of three grown children and currently lives in the Princeton, New Jersey area with his wife, Judy. In his spare time, he is an active volunteer with the American Cancer Society where he helped create **Run for Dad,** a Father's Day event designed to raise awareness about prostate cancer which regularly draws thousands of participants.